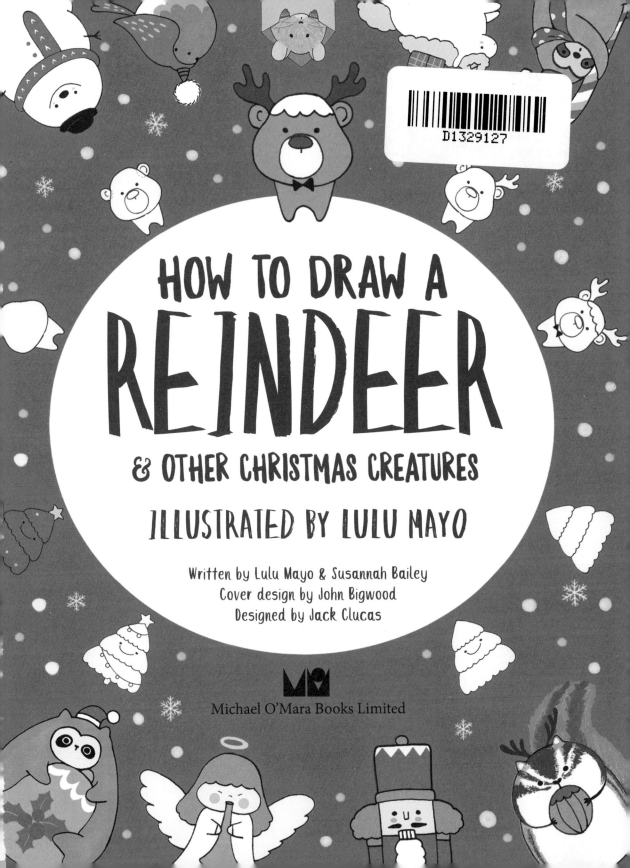

HOW TO DRAW A
REINDEER
& OTHER CHRISTMAS CREATURES

ILLUSTRATED BY LULU MAYO

Written by Lulu Mayo & Susannah Bailey
Cover design by John Bigwood
Designed by Jack Clucas

Michael O'Mara Books Limited

FROM LULU

I hope you love the festive season as much as I do. Inside this book, I'll show you how to draw all the things that make Christmas the most wonderful time of year. This includes snowmen, reindeer, presents and, of course, Santa.

Each magical creation is brought to life in five simple steps, using shapes that are easy to master. Don't worry if you make a mistake or your pictures look different to mine – all drawings are unique and that's part of what makes them special. Have fun!

LULU MAYO

THE STEPS

The clear, step-by-step instructions for
each creation in this book are easy to follow.

Outlining the body & head
gives you a great starting
point. Use a pencil to create
your initial drawing.

1.

Add simple shapes to
start bringing your
work to life.

2.

3.

Add all of the elements.
Then rub out the pencil
lines you don't need.

4.

Go over the outline
in pen if you like.

5.

Finally,
add colour.

NOW PICK
UP YOUR PENCIL
AND DRAW!

SANTA CLAUS

1. start with a triangle
& a fluffy beard

2. add a face, semicircle nose
& dots for eyes & mouth

3. rectangle body, with
triangles for arms & legs

4. draw in buttons
& a belt

5. colour him in

Draw your Santa here.

Santa Claus is coming to town. Fill the page with Santas, including some poking out of chimneys.

Well, this is embarrassing.

REINDEER

1. pear-shaped head
& tooth-shaped body

2. dots for eyes, oval for nose,
circles for ears & snout

3. add antlers

4. add hair & bow tie

5. fill with colour

Now, you try.

Fill the sky with more reindeer.

CHRISTMAS TREE

1. three triangles with
wavy bottoms

2. add dots for eyes &
a curved line for the smile

3. rectangle for the trunk
& a star on top

4. decorate the tree

5. colour it up

Have a go.

Turn this page into a Christmas forest.
Don't forget to dress up all the trees.

HEDGEHOG

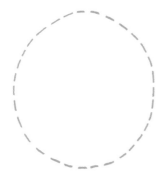

1. start with an oval outline for the body

2. heart for face, circles for ears & eyes, oval nose & lines for claws

3. add a scarf

4. make it really spiky

5. colour it in

Your turn.

Doodle lots of hedgehogs in different poses.
Use the shapes below to help you get started.

It's party time!

SNOWMAN

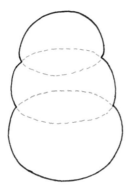

1. three ovals

2. cute facial
expression

3. sticks for hands
& ovals for shoes

4. hat, scarf & buttons

5. add some colour

Draw your own.

Get creative! Draw different faces on to these snowpeople.

CAT

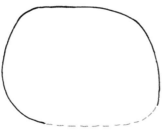

1. start with a
rounded rectangle

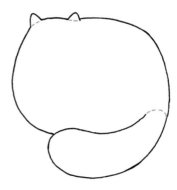

2. triangles for ears
& a sausage tail

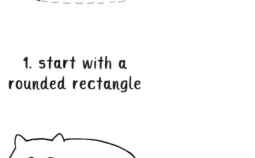

3. eyes, nose & whiskers

4. add ribbon

5. finish with a fun pattern

Give it a go!

Play with simple shapes to create more Christmas cats.
Why not wrap them up as well?

Zzzz ... cat nap.

BADGER BAUBLE

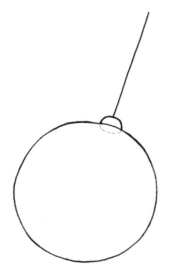

1. start with a line,
oval & circle

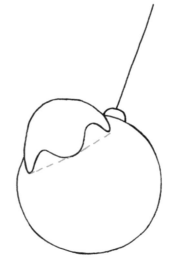

2. add a semicircle
with a wavy line for
head & hands

3. circles for ears,
dots for eyes & mouth
& oval for nose

4. rounded triangles
for legs & oval for tail

5. add black markings
& decorate

Now it's your turn.

Draw a collection of Christmas decorations.

I'm having a ball.

Doodle more fun patterns.

PANDA PRESENT

1. start with a
square & semicircle

2. add ovals for eyes &
nose & semicircles for ears

3. chubby triangular hands
& reindeer antler headband

4. tilted rectangle for lid

5. finish with a jazzy pattern

Have a try!

Draw more presents, then wrap them
all up. What pattern will you pick?

SLOTH

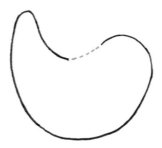

1. banana-shaped body

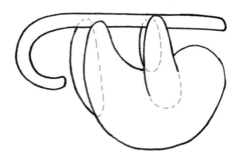

2. long ovals for arms
& legs & a candy cane

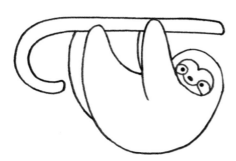

3. heart-shaped face
& smiley expression

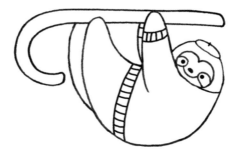

4. draw a beret
& Christmas jumper

5. add some festive colour

Create a sloth here.

Draw more festive sloths. Try using the left oval for
a hanging sloth & the right oval for a do-nothing sloth.

Hanging sloth

Do-nothing sloth

Cuddly
sloth

GINGERBREAD

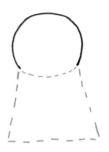

1. circle for the head &
a trapezoid for the body

2. add oval hands & legs

3. circles for eyes, sausage
for mouth & eyebrows

4. add bow tie & hat
& dress it up

5. add a pop of colour

Give it a try.

Experiment with these shapes to create lots of different gingers.

Stripy

Smiley

Happy

Bitten

UNICORN

1. start with three ovals

2. chubby triangles for legs,
clouds for mane & tail

3. dots for eyes & nose
& a stripy horn

4. add presents

5. finish with magical colour

Draw your own.

Doodle more unicorns & horses. Add twinkly lights
& presents to make them extra Christmassy.

I've always
wanted a horn!

HAMSTER

1. a rounded,
upside-down heart

2. add dots for eyes & a
heart-shaped nose & mouth

3. circles for ears, triangles
for legs & lines for claws

4. add a santa hat

5. add markings
& colour it up

Sketch your own.

Use these shapes to draw more cute Christmas hamsters.

I hope you like it.

ELF

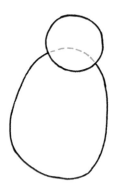

1. circle for head
   & oval for body

2. add eyes, nose,
   mouth & wavy
   line for fringe

3. triangles for
   arms, legs & shoes,
   rectangle for collar
   & dots for buttons

4. circle & triangle
   for pointy hat

5. design your own
   outfit & colour it up

Your turn.

Play with circles, triangles & ovals
to create different elf poses.

PENGUIN

1. start with a
pear-shaped body

2. dots for eyes, triangles
for hands & nose

3. beanie, cross for a
belly button & claws

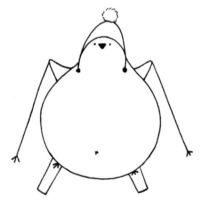

4. rectangles for skis
& lines for poles

5. finish with colour

Doodle your own.

Use these shapes to draw more penguins skiing or carolling.

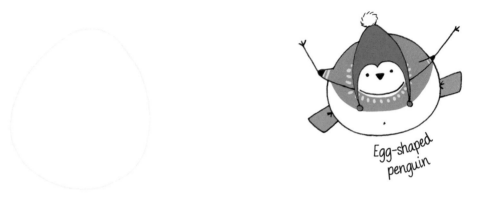

Egg-shaped penguin

Draw your own carolling penguin.

Pear-shaped penguin

Bean-shaped penguin

RUSSIAN DOLL

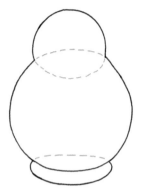

1. two circles for body
& sausage for base

2. circle for face &
wavy line for fringe

3. eyes & mouth

4. add wavy lines

5. finish it with a
festive design

Draw your own doll.

Can you fill the shelves with more Russian dolls or ... animal dolls?

CHIPMUNK

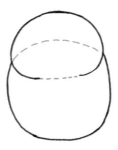

1. two ovals for
head & body

2. add triangles for ears
& a cute expression

3. circle for nut
& lines for claws

4. add tail

5. scribble markings &
make it really fluffy

Give it a go.

Draw more Christmas chipmunks.

I'm stuffed.

MOUSE MAIL

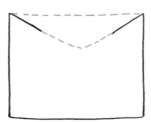

1. rectangle & upside-down
triangle for envelope

2. semicircle for body, furry
semicircle chin & gloves

3. ovals for ears, eyes,
mouth & heart for nose

4. add whiskers & triangle
for back of envelope

5. colour it up

Now it's your turn.

Try creating your mouse with different shapes. Don't forget
to fill the envelope at the bottom with a cute mouse.

ANGEL

1. oval for head, wavy line for fringe & bell-shaped body

2. eyes, hair & semicircle for nose

3. triangles for hands, legs & trumpet

4. add wings

5. colour in

Now you try.

Surround the tree with cute angels. Start with an oval or a
circle & then add a bell or a trapezoid to vary their poses.

That trumpet
sounds terrible.

LLAMA

1. curly hairdo &
fluffy L-shaped body

2. banana-shaped
ears, dots for eyes &
mouth, heart for nose
& circle for muzzle

3. fluffy triangles
for legs & a fluffy
banana-shaped tail

4. draw Christmas
lights & a bow tie

5. add a pop of colour

Doodle your own.

Fill the page with adorable llamas. Why not style them with fun hairdos & Christmas costumes?

Fa-la-la-la-llama

JINGLE RACCOON

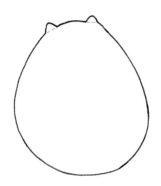

1. egg-shaped body &
triangles for ears

2. heart-shaped face
& cute expression

3. add bell

4. fat triangles for
paws & an oval tail

5. colour it in

Have a go.

Doodle more raccoons swinging on bells.

Ding-dong!

NUTCRACKER

1. rectangle for head & add eyes, nose, moustache & mouth

2. fluffy beard & hair, circle, rounded square & rectangle for hat

3. square & trapezoid for body, rectangle forearms & semicircle hands

4. rectangles for legs & shoes

5. colour it in

Time to try!

Can you fill the shelves with cute nutcrackers?
Try combining different shapes to create your own.

King nutcracker

Drummer nutcracker

OWL

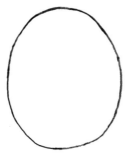

1. oval for body

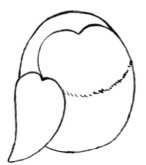

2. hearts for face & wing

3. big eyes, heart for nose & ears

4. add claws & mistletoe

5. complete it with colour

Your turn.

Use the shape to create your own owl,
then draw more owls sitting on mistletoe.

T'wooo are you
looking at?

POLAR BEAR

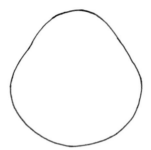

1. chunky pear
shape for body

2. circles for ears, eyes & mouth
& oval for nose & muzzle

3. add hat & gloves

4. ovals for legs &
Christmas jumper collar

5. colour it up

Sketch your own.

Add more polar bears to the snow globe.

FAIRY

1. circle for head, triangles for hand & body

2. cute face, wavy fringe & semicircle for bun

3. ovals for wings & triangles for legs

4. add twinkly candy cane

5. dress her up

Draw your own fairy.

Doodle more adorable flying fairies all over the page.

ROBIN

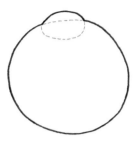

1. oval for head
& circle for body

2. S-shaped wing, dots
for eyes & triangle beak

3. connect the wing &
add heart-shaped tail

4. add hat & ice skates

5. colour it up

Give it a go.

Use these shapes to draw more robins. Try varying the starting shapes to create different poses.

Happy holly-days!

SNOWFLAKE

1. draw a star

2. add dots for
eyes & a smile

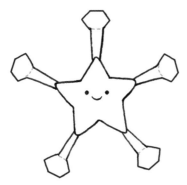

3. draw rectangles
with hexagon ends

4. add rectangles
with oval ends

5. finish with colours

Your turn.

Fill the sky with lots of snowflakes.

Draw a cross, then an X through it to start your drawing.

I'm falling for you.

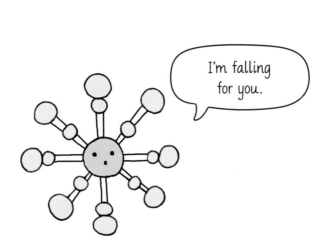

SAUSAGE DOG

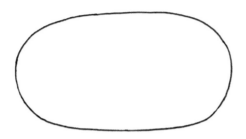

1. sausage shape
for body

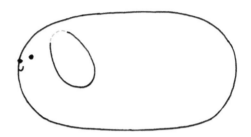

2. eye, nose, mouth
& oval for ear

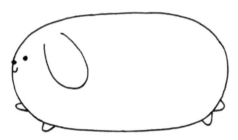

3. triangles
for legs

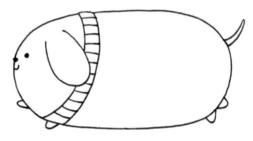

4. add jumper
& tail

5. colour it up

Have a try.

Experiment with these shapes to create more sausage dogs.

GINGERBREAD HOUSE

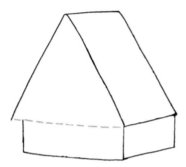

1. triangle & tilted
rectangles

2. add frosting
& a face

3. semicircle windows
& oval door

4. semicircle roof tiles

5. decorate it
however you like

Give it a go.

Build more gingerbread houses in the snowy village.

Welcome!

RABBIT STAR

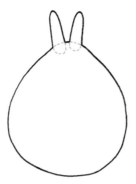

1. egg shape for body
& ovals for ears

2. eyes, nose & beanie

3. triangles for hands,
legs & star

4. add furry tail

5. colour it up

Create your own.

Fill the space with more stars & rabbits. Can you experiment with different shiny-star patterns?

Time to shine!

WREATH

1. doughnut outline,
ribbon & decorations

2. add pine needles

3. oval for fox's body
& very bushy tail

4. triangles for ears
& zigzag mane

5. dots for eyes &
nose & colour it up

Doodle your own.

Design your Christmas wreaths. Don't forget
to decorate them with ribbons & lights.

W www.lulumayo.com   f @lulumayoart   @lulu_mayo_art

First published in Great Britain in 2020 by Michael O'Mara Books Limited,
9 Lion Yard, Tremadoc Road, London SW4 7NQ

W www.mombooks.com
f Michael O'Mara Books
@OMaraBooks

Copyright © 2020 by Lulu Mayo

A CIP catalogue record for this book is available from the British Library.

ISBN: 978-1-78929-243-5

2 4 6 8 10 9 7 5 3 1

This book was printed in China.